Deep Inside that Rounded World

poems by

Shannon Carriger

Finishing Line Press
Georgetown, Kentucky

Deep Inside that Rounded World

Copyright © 2019 by Shannon Carriger
ISBN 978-1-64662-305-1 First Edition
All rights reserved under International and Pan-American Copyright Conventions. No part of this book may be reproduced in any manner whatsoever without written permission from the publisher, except in the case of brief quotations embodied in critical articles and reviews.

ACKNOWLEDGMENTS

I am grateful to the following journals for previously publishing some of the poems in this chapbook:

"Empire" first appeared in *Inscape Magazine*, 2015; winner of the 2015 Editor's Choice Award for poetry.

"Suspension" first appeared in *Midwest Quarterly*, Vol. 55, Issue 4, Summer 2014.

Publisher: Leah Maines
Editor: Christen Kincaid
Cover Art: Taton Tubbs, https://www.facebook.com/Through-My_Eyes-411726422252029/
Author Photo: Shannon Carriger
Cover Design: Elizabeth Maines McCleavy

Order online: www.finishinglinepress.com
also available on amazon.com

Author inquiries and mail orders:
Finishing Line Press
P. O. Box 1626
Georgetown, Kentucky 40324
U. S. A.

Table of Contents

Easement 1

Empire 2

Bishop Rock 3

Ha Long Bay 4

Contrition 5

God's Eye 6

Driving Up Belmont, 1980 7

The Heart's Telegraphy 8

Second Favorite Class 9

Suspension 10

Lena on the Bally-Box 11

Displacement 13

Apposition 14

Angela Addresses the Abbott 15

The Profumo Affair 16

To Samson 17

Deep Inside that Rounded World 18

Persephone 19

Another Guilty Offering 20

Last Year's Anything 21

The Meeting, Washington D.C., 1865 22

Wolves 23

Dissection 24

A Dream 25

Year's End 26

Easement

A barrier against Kansas wind,
my fence fixes limits,
a perimeter established by
posts and braces, sixteen boards
per each eight feet.

One has lost a tooth; its small gap
in the uniform rows letting in
a little more light,
breaking the symmetry of cedar
as winter wheat grows wild
along the easement of separated space.

This is all a year is. An open door
defined by what happens
on the other side. Color and light,
regret and hope.

An empty gap reverently trafficking
in what has been and what yet will be.

Empire
> *For Shoichi Yokoi, a sergeant in the Japanese Imperial Army during WWII*

By twenty-five, he could tell a man's inseam
without unrolling his tape. His small eyes,
silver-black, noted the heft of hipbones,
waist width, the elegant angle of ankles.

His Japan was not sword sharp, a knife blade
expertly pressed against an enemy throat,
a black robe full of precise and persistent
revenge, blousy with tradition.

By twenty-six, he was a soldier, measuring
steps instead of seams, dreaming of war
instead of shirtwaist dresses, a severed limb
encased in a perfect dolman sleeve.

His Japan was linen and silk, cotton and
tweed, dancers' skirts and grandfathers'
fine gold buttons marching up and down
bolts he touched each day with tender fingers.

By twenty-eight, he was in hiding, stitching
his silence into cave walls with torn nails,
his heart the red blood dot pulsing in the
Japanese flag, a button blinking back the darkness.

Bishop Rock

In the 13th century, the rock was a prison
for felons, dropped to live with little food
or water until the sea swept them back to God.

Five hundred years later, shipwrecks. Invisible
in dark water, the rock split skiffs, splintering what
was once whole into halves. Everything goes in time.

Bones soften, gums erode, eyelashes fall out, nothing
can hold back the inevitable wreckage of a body.

1858 brought the lighthouse, a beacon marking distance,
staving off the break down, where two keepers ten floors
above the Atlantic needed no one but each other.

They were dropped onto the island to be the light
in the darkness, to steer the lost towards home, knowing
everything in time would go, until God swept them both away.

Ha Long Bay

Some 1600 rock islands litter
water like raised middle fingers
pointed toward an almost too blue sky.

The rest of the fist rests, buried beneath
a cerulean sea that never apologizes
for damage done out of sight.

Called karst, these rocks
occur naturally, unlike war.
There is no menace in these monoliths.

Starless skies mask the monsters,
as the unknowing crack up against
the rock. Just another casualty.

In sunlight, bright green strings
of houseboats huddle, carving out
a home, one squid net at a time.

Ha Long Bay, exotic as calamari,
crunchy-soft, salty, something
I crave without understanding.

My father, who loves water, didn't
wander North enough to see it, spending
instead his eighteenth summer in country.

Fighting a war he didn't understand,
eyes almost too blue, he huddled
in the jungle, praying to come home.

Contrition

Head hidden by black waterfalls of fabric,
a single band of white at her throat,
the nun floats like an angel in reverse

like smoking stalks in fallow fields
like country folk who don't heed ordinances
like a little girl gone giddy over a new dress

like paper worn soft and curling in on itself
like crescent shaped curves of hammered copper
like somehow, her figure will inspire

something other than fear in me.

But, I am no Catholic and this is not Sunday
and someone should have been here an hour
ago to collect my dirty clothes and small tired body,

so I am still sitting here on the concrete
steps of a school I don't go to on a too warm
afternoon and the nun, smiling, doesn't slow down

as she swims forward, her hands in pockets I can't see,
wearing a smile of contrition that seems to apologize
for the hard working father who forgot to pick me up,

secretly smug that her Father never forgets a thing.

God's Eye

My first time at church camp, we made
God's Eyes, yarn-crafted disasters
to take home, a reminder God is with us,
that He is always watching, that we are safe.

My God's Eye didn't work. It didn't make
me think of sacrifice or the comfort of Jesus.
It reminded me of canoeing, the certainty I felt
that the boat would tip, but only I would fall out.

The last night, I walked alone to the bathroom,
a dim yellow light flickering beneath
summer stars. Everyone else was asleep or
paired off like Noah's ark, in twosies-twosies.

After brushing my teeth, I saw the snake,
its body curled like a stack of tires around
the toilet, a reminder there would never be
a place safe enough for danger not to find me.

Driving Up Belmont, 1980

Blazing orange neon blares
Kwik-Shop just before the stop sign
dismisses dashed lines splitting the street,
spitting color onto concrete and passing cars.

Twin skaters loom to the left on gray
brick, his rolled shirtsleeves and her skirt
a nod to years before when the rink
was built, to before most of us were here.

They flank the drive-in at the edge
of town, girded from behind by simple
pine, no support beams to hold up
the whole Technicolor world.

Tonight, the moon is a Ferris wheel
beside the screen, orange as winter wheat,
teaching me at four-years-old what it means
to feel tiny and giant at the same time.

The Heart's Telegraphy
For Samuel Morse who invented the telegraph in 1832

Morse had an affinity for structure,
things grown from ground, something
where there was nothing.

He knew his Greek and Latin, knew
the curves of roots and their anchored
intentions, war-full and peace-empty
in the name of new language.

Long before the tap tap tapping,
his wife—sicker than he'd known—
clutched sheets, her speech gone,
trying to hold on until he
could gallop his way home.

In his hurried too-late hoofbeats
to her, he heard the code. Shy shorts
brushing brightly against longer lengths,
the rhythm of his heart's telegraphy,

an undercurrent to the miles
beyond mountains he'd
have no reason to cross again.

Second Favorite Class

For weeks he tries to teach
me French, small phrases
he's learning upstairs
in another room
from another woman
just as worn out as I am.

This is a boy with a smell.
The dusty-must of poverty
with a dash of obesity's
tang that lingers on the armchair
he borrows each day, fearing
the cheap plastic ones under
the asses of everyone else
will give out beneath his own.

He likes me, he says,
this boy who is, on paper,
a study in failure. Classes
he's failed and family who've
failed him and a system
that pushes him through
when he needs to fail and stay put.

Just after asking to use the bathroom—
Je peux aller à la salle de bain?—
he says mine is his second favorite class.

I hope he does not fail this year.
I hope I do not fail him.
I hope he washes his hands.

Suspension

While designing the bridge, hunched over his work
table like an arthritic old woman, his broad back

humped and hands rigid from sketching and erasing
fine lines, calculating cable tension and compression,

the architect dreams in numbers. Eyes heavy in the yellow
glow of lamplight, breath rattling like baby teeth in glass jars,

he figures the cans and cannots of construction: pounds of
pressure per inch, the elegant transfer of weight to ground.

He has built bridges before, fortified with falsework,
intricate timber arms supporting unstable structures, but,

lately, he has tired of their need and wants, instead,
to sway kite-like in strong wind, accepting he may fall.

Suspension bridges grow out like climbing vines, taut tendrils
seeking separate shores, easily reaching to span space.

Each day, now, the architect lays a few more feet of ground knowing
soon it will be done and he will walk, one last time, to the other side.

Lena on the Bally Box
    After a photograph by Susan Meiselas

I.
It's been four years since
the Olympics when Lena
held her breath and watched
the scraggly-haired American
with the bushy mustache press
into the wind, his body moving
like gears in her grandfather's
watch, arms and legs marking
time around a track that would,
eventually, beat him.

Four years since graduation,
four years remembering track stars
with quick feet and ropey arms
to pin a girl against cracked
back seat vinyl til she was
dreamily defenseless.

Those boys knew about stamina.
They held their breath and kissed
with their eyes open to see the finish
line instead of groping for it in the dark.

Those boys were gone, running out
of town almost before their
graduation caps hit the ground.

II.
A week ahead of the carnival,
the advance man comes to Guthrie.
Scraggly-haired and bushy mustached,
a smile with as much grease as teeth,
Billy Howard comes to pay off cops,
secure licenses, chat up local girls
with nothing but Guthrie Beauty School
or disappointing marriages to look forward
to, their best days behind them. He needs
girls for the strong show and knows
moony eyes and broken hearts
are best for that kind of work.

III.
Lena's been flying for a week or so. Drowsy
from the drugs someone always has
on hand, she squints at the lights, those
false stars, and tells herself it's not so bad.

Summer is long, and from up here Billy
could be the Olympic runner who died last year.

She shakes on her box, sleepily spinning
as she tries to break the land speed record.

Every night she dreams of running.

Displacement

Slick with sea salt
from the separating bath,
Archimedes found it first,
his weight and weariness
displacing the wet.
Testing his theory
with rocks and crowns,
he saw truth repeated:
as the line rose, each new
object had its way with water.

Bruised or brushed by love,
the human heart displaces
nothing. Heavy beating
in a hurried chest or dead-dropped
into chemical jars, it cannot help
but float, feather light and fervid,
in its need to keep expanding.

Apposition

After a photograph of Marianne Faithfull taken by
Gered Mankowitz in 1964

Your great-great uncle gave his name
to masochism, Marianne.
Even when you were eighteen,
exposed,
screwing yourself famous,
you must have known it.

Mankowitz swears you were like this
when he found you—
a dazed doll in a polyester print—
posing.
Your crossed legs lucent
in the lurid light of Salisbury Pub.

The camera caught the figure eight
of your body—
your oblique arms outstretched—
opposite
to the public perception of you
as a cold, closed thing.

Your face is a refraction of the light
above and within you, Marianne.
It curves deferentially in an attempt at
apposition:
your name in the same breath
as Edie, Sara, and all the other darlings.

Angela Addresses the Abbess
For Angela de Foligno, a thirteenth century mystic

At thirty-seven, I'll repent. Give my beauty
back to the vestal virgin and keep my legs closed.

Until then though, sister, let me welcome
all manner of men into my soft salvation.

Give me gravediggers, nails dark with dirt
and death, clutching life in me like a spade.

Give me bakers, hands softer than calf-skin,
watching my rise and fall with rapt attention.

Give me the Pope, his robes ready to drop
like the lowered lashes of a school girl.

Then, when God and plague have taken
mother, husband, sons, I'll give myself to Him.

At thirty-seven, I'll give Him the body I no
longer need, an old shoe with no foot left to fit it.

The Profumo Affair

For Christine Keeler who had an affair with a married
English government minister in 1962

Between the dress shop and the sergeant,
I learned what others liked in me.

Helpful to know things like that when a baby
dies after six days and you're only seventeen.

Her feet whistling the day she shipped me
off, swift as she saw me to the door,

Mum called me a right woman, setting us
both free with one cheap train ticket.

So off to London, to Murray's, to showing my bits,
and to Stephen who never wanted to sleep with me,

bending and stretching me, instead, into shapes
for paint until I was only angles, awkward and acrylic.

Then, of course, came John, the Peter to my Christ.

I loved him a little until he denied me, and then

I loved him more.

To Samson
> *"So Delilah said to Samson, 'Tell me the secret of your great strength.'"*
> —Judges 16:6

Outside, soldiers wait
for my whisper
at the window,
their heads itchy
with dark dreams
of your blood, my body.

I wait for your arrival,
the barren earth
crackling beneath
your warrior feet,
my heart twittering
like a thousand birds.

Bring me your
murderous hands, rough
with God's work.
Lie still as I press
my face to your chest,
songs of angels ringing
in your righteous blood.

Trust my words,
promises only possible
from a fatherless girl.
Listen for my song
of betrayal: my small
omissions, my
sweet silences.

Know I am sorry for this.

Deep Inside that Rounded World
"Sarah said, 'God has brought me laughter…'"
—*Genesis 21:6*

Sarah knew the value of waiting for ripeness,
the promise of texture and consistency buried
beneath the skin of a well-timed peach.

Not hers to bear, she watched Hagar's belly,
heavy with fruit, the secret sweetness hidden
deep inside that rounded world.

But Hagar's baby didn't sate Sarah, so she
begged every day for a fig of her own until
the morning she found herself swelling.

Abraham brought her a basket of dates as she
marveled at her miracle. Throwing her head back
laughing, she ate them slowly, her mouth full of joy.

Persephone

The terrible truth of the underworld
is that it is not terrible at all.

A girl can be crowned queen there,
a scepter where her sewing had been.

When mama heard of my abduction,
she stopped earth's spinning. That's

the thing about mothers: they'll
starve the world to save their own.

Uncle H sent me back, of course, but not
before slipping me those seven seeds

that stained my teeth and bound me
to him: ox and cart, needle and thread.

Returning, mama wanted me innocent,
all narcissus and naps and knitting.

Blaming him for my new taste for the dark,
she disliked me as a woman grown.

Gleaning me on gardens and raising
me to suspect resurrection, she shouldn't

have been surprised when, after
the underworld, I longed to be immortal.

Another Guilty Offering

*For Hannah Duston, taken captive during
King Williams's War in 1697*

Shoulders bare, waved hair pulled back,
Hannah Duston demands attention just
off Commercial St. Even granite fails
to harden the curves beneath her slipping dress.

The first American woman immortalized
in stone is on a pedestal alone, her dress draped
in Grecian creases against a bent knee, her
sightless eyes fixed on an uncertain horizon.

In 1697, Hannah'd had her ninth child. Three
days later, Abenaki bore down on her farm,
marching her miles away, leaving safely
behind her husband and other eight.

The baby died when its head met tree-bark,
smashed perhaps by a warrior tired of white
settlers claiming his home as theirs, tired
of burying his own dead. Tired.

Escape meant murder, so Hannah slaughtered
ten and was statued for it. Tomahawk in her
right hand, a scalp bouquet in her left, she stands,
another guilty offering to the New World.

Last Year's Anything
> *"What is last year's snow to me?*
> *Last year's anything?"*
> —Countee Cullen

The church in '28, a congregation
of caged birds atwitter with words unsaid,
watched him wed in orchid heavy air.

All of Harlem and the court of Negritude
turned out to witness the creation
of the new, his name tied to a woman

who did not believe the rumors
until he spoke the words himself.

His lover, in '42, a silent, focused saint,
eyed the camera so intensely, Cullen must
have felt seen from space.

Countee must have felt the doors open
if only for a minute, some phantom ghosting
past convention, filling his lungs so full

the songs he sang just might could have reached
o'er Jordan, if only he'd opened his mouth.

The Meeting, Washington D.C., 1865
For Walt Whitman and Peter Doyle

Ample it was, the rain, sufficient proof
that water, spiritual and eternal, currents
forever curling, curious and sensual,
seeking out the source, can and will
reveal the immaculate infinite world.

Collar open, Adonis at the wheel,
hair heavy in a face made for framing,
Peter stared without ceasing, etching
into memory the other man, maneuvering
the car from Capitol to Treasury.

Imagine the miracle of them, momentary
and momentous, alone in lamp-glow,
the car a humming heart on rain-slick streets,
empty of traffic, empty of man, empty
of any soul save these two together.

Blanket-shouldered and weary, the last
in a day's worth of riders smelled of
salt and sweat, blue eyes electric beneath
the broad brimmed hat so out of fashion,
his beard pulsing in the car's red light.

Young and lonely and tired and cold,
Peter came to sit, wordless and wondering
at the work of forty-five years, their breath
thick between them, honey-drunk as bees
after a dizzy day among the lilacs.

Only twenty-one, he placed his conductor's
hand on the knobbed knee of America,
calloused and rough it was and strong,
and all was made white and beautiful,
the universe scrubbed clean. They knew.

Wolves
> *"I want there always to be wolves. Always, always."*
> —Trapper Mike Johnson

As a child, he wanted
to love them,
to open wide his tiny arms
as their lips pulled
back, their black gums
giving way to teeth
sharpened on smaller
animal bones, his little
boy heart too big to fear them.

He doesn't try to love
them now, to hold
their soft ferocity
in his cracked hands
as the heat of their skin
rises like so many
secrets, their animal smell
mixing with his own.

Time makes trappers
of even the bravest boys.

He's learned the only
safe howl comes like
a choked bird's song
from his own chest:

the only animal
he can love,
and still survive.

Dissection

My lab partner steals baby sharks from the belly
of another because, she says, ours should
know motherhood, even if it is post-mortem.

She spends hours determining the dominant,
reading the recessive, convinced she can plan
a perfect child through intentional design.

I have no interest in taking things apart,
no interest in where my green eyes came from
or why my father lost his hair so young.

Hands inside the dead shark, holding babies
that don't belong, I see this is no lesson of
beginning. It feels too much like the end.

A Dream
For Seamus Heaney

Last night, I fell asleep
while reading you.

In the dark, I walked
through briar and brickyard,

long hair down my back
in a thick red plait, my

fingers stained with
the juice of blackberries.

Leaning over the lip
of a well, I searched

the deep but saw
no reflection and heard

no echo. Were it not
for the fact of morning,

I would still be there,
looking down.

Year's End
> *(This is the school in which we learn ...)*
> —Delmore Schwartz

Slog and moor and dusky edges be damned
in this space, both cell and sanctuary, more than
the best have had. Pound in Pisa, mad
scratching the cage until his mind, un-dammed,
broke so far open that even in D.C. the man
he had been couldn't come back. Sad

to think we lose ourselves here, too. Cinder
walls in graywash, a wasteland even Sexton
couldn't renew. Tied to failure's anvil, all
illusion, delicate as wrist-skin, ended with her,
back to Bedlam where her swimming began,
nothing left but her silhouette, her words, her fall.

Milton-blind perhaps we are, here in this antique
box. Our books too high, our language faltering
when we need it most, sly truth and gaudy lies
tied in the three-legged-race to year's end, weak.
No matter how lost this paradise, erring
as it does some days, I still choose it, and you, besides.

Additional Acknowledgments

My heartfelt gratitude to Greg LeGault, Linda Lewis, and Susan Jackson Rodgers who taught me far more than the content of their courses. I am indebted to Jamie Heller and Bill Patterson for their keen eyes and patience as readers and as friends, and to Jamie Johnson who never fails to amaze me with the depth of her kindness and the breadth of her love.

I am thankful for my parents, Paul and Linda, who always listen when I have something to say, and for my brother Brandon, my first and oldest friend.

And finally to Michael who makes me safe, keeps me sane, and reminds me to breathe. Without you, my good, good man, this book and the life I love so much wouldn't exist.

Shannon Carriger has a box full of journals she kept through middle school, high school, college, and into adulthood. Some feature floral covers, pressed flowers, and hot pink ink; others include lists of books she loves and people she does not. All include poetry, her first love, which she writes whenever she can. Passionately devoted to the beauty of words, Carriger has built a life around the reading, writing, and study of literature.

In 2015, she was awarded the Editor's Choice Award for Poetry and was nominated for a Pushcart Prize by *Inscape Magazine*. Her work has appeared in several publications including *Manhattan Book Review, Midwest Quarterly, Kansas English,* and *Cathexis Northwest Press*. Carriger makes her home in Ottawa, KS, with her best friend and love of her life, Michael.

www.ingramcontent.com/pod-product-compliance
Lightning Source LLC
LaVergne TN
LVHW041515070426
835507LV00012B/1597